Crime and Courts Bill [HL]

SIXTH
MARSHALLED
LIST OF AMENDMENTS
TO BE MOVED
IN COMMITTEE
OF THE WHOLE HOUSE

The amendments have been marshalled in accordance with the Instruction of 12th June 2012, as follows—

Clauses 24 to 26   Clause 23
Schedule 14   Clause 28
Clause 27   Schedule 16
Schedule 15   Clauses 29 to 31

[*Amendments marked ★ are new or have been altered*]

Amendment No.

Clause 24

LORD AVEBURY

148A   Page 23, line 2, at end insert—

"( )   This section shall not have effect in relation to an appeal against a refusal of entry clearance where that decision was taken wholly or partly on a general ground for refusal in rules as laid by the Secretary of State for the purposes of section 1(4) of the Immigration Act 1971."

Lord Avebury gives notice of his intention to oppose the Question that Clause 24 stand part of the Bill.

| Amendment No. | After Clause 24 |

LORD AVEBURY

148B   Insert the following new Clause—

"Immigration appeals: race discrimination grounds

In the Nationality, Immigration and Asylum Act 2002, in section 84(1)(b), after "Race Relations (Northern Ireland) Order 1997" insert "or relates to section 115 of the Equality Act 2010 in relation to the protected characteristic identified in section 9 of that Act"."

148C   Insert the following new Clause—

"Immigration appeals: asylum and humanitarian protection

In the Nationality, Immigration and Asylum Act 2002, in section 83(1)(b) omit the words from "Kingdom" to the end."

148D   Insert the following new Clause—

"Appeal from within the United Kingdom: unfounded human rights or asylum claim

In the Nationality, Immigration and Asylum Act 2002, in section 94, omit subsection (8)."

148E   Insert the following new Clause—

"Appeal in progress

In the Nationality, Immigration and Asylum Act 2002, in section 99(1), omit "96(1) or (2)"."

Clause 25

LORD AVEBURY

148F   Page 23, line 22, at end insert—

"(4)   This section does not apply if—

       (a)   the person concerned is stateless,

       (b)   the person concerned has previously made an asylum claim or a human rights claim and been granted leave on that basis, or

       (c)   the person concerned asserts in his or her grounds of appeal an asylum claim or a human rights claim."

148G   [*Withdrawn*]

LORD HENLEY
LORD AVEBURY

149   Page 23, line 23, leave out subsection (4)

| Amendment No. | Clause 25—*continued* |

LORD AVEBURY

Lord Avebury gives notice of his intention to oppose the Question that Clause 25 stand part of the Bill.

After Clause 25

LORD AVEBURY

149A   Insert the following new Clause—

> **"Amendment of the Legal Aid, Sentencing and Punishment of Offenders Act 2012**
>
> In Schedule 1 to the Legal Aid, Sentencing and Punishment of Offenders Act 2012, after paragraph 30 insert—
>
> *"Immigration: civil legal services provided in relation to certain variations of leave*
>
> 30A   Civil legal services provided in relation to a decision under section 82(2)(e) of the Nationality, Immigration and Asylum Act 2002 in cases where the Secretary of State seeks to rely on section 97B of that Act.""

149B   Insert the following new Clause—

> **"Immigration and nationality appeals from the Upper Tribunal**
>
> Section 13(6) of the Tribunals, Courts and Enforcement Act 2007 (right of appeal to Court of Appeal etc.) does not apply in relation to immigration and nationality appeals from the Upper Tribunal."

149C   Insert the following new Clause—

> **"Immigration and nationality appeals from the Upper Tribunal**
>
> (1) Section 13(6) of the Tribunals, Courts and Enforcement Act 2007 (right of appeal to the Court of Appeal etc.) does not apply in relation to immigration and nationality appeals from the Upper Tribunal where the grounds of appeal include a point of law relating to the Refugee Convention or the Human Rights Convention.
>
> (2) In this section—
>
> > "the Refugee Convention" means the Convention relating to the Status of Refugees done at Geneva on 28th July 1951 and its Protocol;
> >
> > "the Human Rights Convention" has the same meaning as "the Convention" in the Human Rights Act 1998."

Amendment No.	Clause 26

BARONESS SMITH OF BASILDON
LORD ROSSER
LORD BEECHAM

149CA Page 23, line 29, at end insert "who is working in Criminal and Financial Investigation"

149CB Page 23, line 41, leave out subsections (4) and (5)

LORD BERKELEY

149D Page 25, line 5, at end insert—

"(6A) In the UK Borders Act 2007, in section 48 (establishment) after paragraph (2)(b) insert—

"(c) practice and procedure in facilitating the entry into the UK of all bona fide EU and other passport holders, in monitoring of waiting times for processing of incoming passengers at fixed control points, and in processing passengers on international train services between the nearest stations served on each side of the border.""

LORD HENLEY

150 Page 25, line 23, at end insert ", or

(c) in connection with the prevention, investigation or prosecution of any of the following offences (insofar as that does not involve the exercise of a function which falls within paragraph (a) or (b))—

(i) an offence under section 26(1)(a), (b) or (g) of the Immigration Act 1971 (refusal or failure to submit to examination or to furnish information etc, or obstruction of immigration officer);

(ii) an offence under section 22 of the UK Borders Act 2007 (assaulting an immigration officer)."

151 Page 26, line 8, after "offence" insert "or immigration enforcement offence"

152 Page 26, line 26, at end insert—

""immigration enforcement offence" means any of the following offences (insofar as they are not immigration or nationality offences)—

(a) an offence under section 26(1)(a), (b) or (g) of the Immigration Act 1971 (refusal or failure to submit to examination or to furnish information etc, or obstruction of immigration officer);

(b) an offence under section 22 of the UK Borders Act 2007 (assaulting an immigration officer);"

153 Page 26, line 44, leave out "officers of Revenue and Customs" and insert "immigration officers"

Amendment No.	Clause 26—*continued*

LORD AVEBURY

153A Page 27, line 8, at end insert—

"( ) The Borders, Citizenship and Immigration Act 2009 is amended as follows—

    (a) in section 23(1) for "the Secretary of State must" substitute "the Secretary of State may";

    (b) after section 23(1)(d), insert—

        "(e) the provision of services provided by another person pursuant to arrangements which are made by the Secretary of State and relating to the discharge of a function within paragraphs (a) to (d).""

Schedule 14

BARONESS SMITH OF BASILDON
LORD ROSSER
LORD BEECHAM

153B Page 211, line 2, leave out paragraphs 14 to 39

LORD HENLEY

154 Page 219, line 9, at end insert—

"(4) Regulation 3(1)(b) of the Criminal Legal Assistance (Duty Solicitors) (Scotland) Regulations 2011 (duty solicitors: advice for suspects) applies in relation to a person to whom section 25A of the 1995 Act applies by virtue of its amendment by paragraph 46 of this Schedule; and, accordingly, in regulation 3(1)(b), after "customs" insert ", immigration and nationality".

(5) But regulation 3(1)(b) does not have effect in relation to such a person in a case where—

    (a) the person is detained under section 24 of the 1995 Act, and the period of detention began before the time at which paragraph 46 of this Schedule comes into force;

    (b) the person attends as mentioned in section 25A(1)(d) of the 1995 Act, and the period of attendance began before that time; or

    (c) the person is arrested and detained as mentioned in section 25A(1)(e) of that Act, and the arrest occurred before that time.

(6) Sub-paragraph (4) does not affect the application of regulation 3(1)(b) in relation to a person to whom section 25A of the 1995 Act applies otherwise than by virtue of its amendment by paragraph 47 of this Schedule.

(7) Sub-paragraphs (4) to (6) do not prevent regulation 3(1)(b) from being amended or revoked by exercise of any power conferred by the Legal Aid (Scotland) Act 1986 or any other power.

(8) In this paragraph "1995 Act" means the Criminal Law (Consolidation) (Scotland) Act 1995."

| Amendment No. | Clause 27 |

BARONESS MEACHER

154ZA Page 27, line 18, leave out "controlled"

154ZB Page 27, line 19, after "if" insert—

"(a) D has been involved in a road traffic accident, or

(b) D is in charge of a vehicle and the roadside evidence suggests D is impaired due to alcohol or a drug, and

(c) D is not taking a prescribed medicine,

(d) reliable tests have shown that the level of a drug in D's blood or urine is above the level approved in regulations as presenting no threat to road safety, and"

BARONESS SMITH OF BASILDON
LORD ROSSER
LORD BEECHAM

154ZC Page 27, leave out lines 25 to 29

BARONESS HAMWEE

154A Page 27, line 26, leave out from "supplied" to ", and" in line 29

BARONESS SMITH OF BASILDON
LORD ROSSER
LORD BEECHAM

154AA Page 27, line 37, leave out paragraph (a) and insert—

"(a) knowingly contrary to any advice (which may take account of any accompanying instructions given by the manufacturer or distributor of the drug), given by the person by whom the drug was prescribed or supplied, about the amount of time that should elapse between taking the drug and driving a motor vehicle"

154AB Page 27, leave out lines 41 to 43

BARONESS HAMWEE

154B Page 28, line 12, at end insert "following consultation with the Advisory Council on the Misuse of Drugs, persons representing the medical profession, the pharmaceutical industry, and patients and other appropriate persons"

154C Page 28, line 16, at end insert—

"( ) In this section "supplied" includes purchased over the counter."

BARONESS MEACHER

154CA Page 28, leave out line 17

Crime and Courts Bill [HL]

| Amendment No. | Clause 27—*continued* |

BARONESS HAMWEE

154D Page 28, leave out line 17 and insert—

"( ) Limits specified under subsection (2) may be different for—

(a) a drug prescribed or supplied for medical or dental purposes, and

(b) controlled drugs."

BARONESS MEACHER

154DA Page 28, line 20, leave out paragraph (a)

Baroness Meacher gives notice of her intention to oppose the Question that Clause 27 stand part of the Bill.

After Clause 27

LORD MAWHINNEY
LORD MACKAY OF CLASHFERN
LORD MACDONALD OF RIVER GLAVEN
BARONESS HAMWEE
[*Amendment 155 was formerly numbered 79*]

155 Insert the following new Clause—

"Public order

Public order offences

(1) Section 5 of the Public Order Act 1986 is amended as follows.

(2) In subsection (1), for "abusive or insulting" in the two places where it occurs there is substituted "or abusive"."

Clause 23

LORD RAMSBOTHAM

Lord Ramsbotham gives notice of his intention to oppose the Question that Clause 23 stand part of the Bill.

Clause 28

LORD HENLEY
LORD McNALLY

155A Page 29, line 23, after "State" insert "or Lord Chancellor"

155B Page 29, line 28, after "State" insert "or Lord Chancellor"

155C Page 29, line 38, at end insert—

"(ea) an order under section 22(1);"

155CA [*Withdrawn*]

Clause 28—*continued*

LORD HENLEY
LORD McNALLY

155D Page 29, line 42, after "State" insert "or Lord Chancellor"

155E Page 30, line 21, leave out subsections (9) and (10)

Clause 31

LORD AVEBURY

155F Page 31, line 30, at end insert—

"( ) An order to bring section 26 into force shall not be made until—

(a) the Secretary of State has laid before Parliament a report about training, supervision and regulation of immigration officers;

(b) the Secretary of State has confirmed that she is satisfied that the training and supervision provided to immigration officers is adequate to allow them to fulfil their duties; and

(c) the Secretary of State has confirmed that provisions of a code have been specified for the purposes of section 145(1) of the Immigration and Asylum Act 1999 in relation to immigration officers exercising any of the powers to which that section refers."

LORD HENLEY
LORD McNALLY

156 Page 31, line 35, after "1920" insert ", in sections 8(4) and 33(3) of the Maintenance Orders (Reciprocal Enforcement) Act 1972"

157 Page 31, line 36, at end insert—

"(7A) The amendments made by this Act in the Industrial and Provident Societies Act 1965 extend to England and Wales, and Scotland, only."

158 Page 31, line 37, leave out "subsection (7)" and insert "subsections (7) and (7A)"

159 Page 31, line 39, at end insert—

"(8A) Subsection (8) does not apply to the amendments made by this Act in the Government Annuities Act 1929 or the Friendly Societies Act 1974 (which amendments, accordingly, extend to England and Wales, Scotland and Northern Ireland only)."

Crime and Courts Bill [HL]

SIXTH

MARSHALLED

LIST OF AMENDMENTS

TO BE MOVED

IN COMMITTEE

OF THE WHOLE HOUSE

2nd July 2012

PUBLISHED BY AUTHORITY OF THE HOUSE OF LORDS
LONDON — THE STATIONERY OFFICE LIMITED

£2·50